Slow Cooking for Two:

Best Simple and Deliciously Healthy Recipes for 2016

Author: Rebecca Lacey

Contents

Contents

Introduction

I want to thank you and congratulate you for downloading the book, *"Slow Cooking for Two: Best Simple and Deliciously Healthy Recipes"*.

The thing about slow cooking is that you really need to have patience for it. After all, it's not like you're just going to put a dish inside the oven and expect that it'll turn out great in just five minutes or so.

But, the great thing about slow-cooked dishes is that they are the kind of dishes that you'd really love to eat. They're carefully crafted, and have been cooked to perfection!

With the help of this book, you'll learn how to cook the best slow-cooked meals for two! From easy to cook, fresh recipes, to how to transform leftovers, recipes for 3 ½ quart slow cookers, vegan or gluten free options, and slow cooked meals for two—you'll find them all right here.

Read this book now and start cooking.

Thanks again for downloading this book, I hope you enjoy it!

Don't forget to like Slow Cooker Meals For Two on Facebook!

https://www.facebook.com/Slowcookingfortwo/

To purchase the next book in this series:
"Daniel Fast: The Ultimate Guide to Slow Cooker Meals for Breakfast, Lunch, and Dinner for 2016 - Dairy Free & Vegan**", click <u>HERE</u>**

https://amzn.com/B01DI3INUO

Chapter 1: Easy-to-Prep, Fresh, and Flavorful Recipes

Slow Cooking, especially for beginners, could be fun when you make use of fresh and flavorful ingredients to create easy to prepare—but definitely delicious dishes. You'll find some in this chapter.

Slow-Cooked Jambalaya

Prep: 10 minutes
Cook: 8 hours 2 minutes (low) / 3 to 4 hours (high)

Ingredients:
1 lb boneless and skinless chicken halves cut into cubes
1 can tomatoes, diced and juiced
1 lb sausage, sliced
1 cup chicken broth
1 cup celery, chopped
1 large onion, chopped
1 lb frozen shrimp, thawed and cooked without tails
½ tsp dried thyme
1 tsp cayenne pepper
2 tsp Cajun Seasoning
2 tsp dried oregano

Instructions:
Mix chicken, tomatoes, sausage, green bell pepper, celery, onion, and broth before adding thyme, cayenne pepper, Cajun seasoning, parsley, and oregano.
Cover the dish and cook accordingly. Add shrimp in the last 30 minutes of cooking time.

Slow-Cooked Cuban Pork and Black Beans

Prep: 15 minutes
Cook: 8 hours, 45 minutes

Ingredients:
¼ cup fresh cilantro, chopped
2 ¾ cups unsalted chicken stock
2 2/3 cup cooked white rice
1 jalapeno pepper, seeded and sliced thinly
1 ½ cups tomatoes, chopped
1 bay leaf
1 ½ tsp crushed red pepper
2 tsp ground cumin
2 tsp paprika
¼ cup fresh oregano, divided
10 garlic cloves, chopped and divided
2 ¼ cups chopped onion, divided
1 lb dried black beans
1 bone-in pork shoulder, trimmed
4 center cut bacon slices, chopped
1 medium orange, quartered
1 ½ tsp freshly ground black pepper
1 cup fresh orange juice
½ cup cilantro stems, chopped

Instructions:

Combine chicken stock, cilantro stems, orange juice, and medium orange in a blender, and pulse until smooth. Add salt and black pepper and then cook bacon until crisp.

Cook pork drippings for 8 minutes in medium high heat. Add pork shoulder, and uncooked black beans.

Add garlic cloves and onion and sauté for 3 minutes. Add crushed red pepper, paprika, oregano, and cumin, and sauté for a minute. Add bay leaf and orange mixture and boil for a minute. Add onion mixture, and then shred pork before discarding the bones.

Add the rest of the ingredients and cook as needed.

Serve and enjoy!

Slow-Cooked Chicken with Oregano, Grape Tomatoes, and Orzo

Prep: 20 minutes
Cook: 2 to 4 hours

Ingredients:
Snipped fresh oregano
1 Tbsp grated Parmesan Cheese
2 Tbsp lemon juice
1 tsp lemon peel, shredded finely
1 ½ cups cooked orzo pasta
2 cups grape tomatoes
1 10 oz pack frozen spinach, thawed and chopped
3 garlic cloves, minced
1 14 ½ oz can reduced-sodium chicken broth
1 Tbsp olive oil
4 8 oz boneless and skinless chicken breasts
1/8 tsp ground black pepper
¼ tsp salt
1 tsp dried parsley, crushed
1 tsp dried basil, crushed
1 tsp dried oregano, crushed

Instructions:

Combine parsley, basil, oregano, salt, and pepper in a bowl and then sprinkle over the chicken. Cook chicken in a large skillet until brown or for at least 6 minutes and then remove from heat.

Combine broth, chicken, and garlic in the bottom of the slow-cooker. Top with tomatoes and add spinach. Cover and cook for at least 2 to 4 hours.

Take the chicken away from the cooker. Cover, and keep warm and then transfer into a large bowl using slotted spoon. Add cooked pasta, lemon juice, and lemon peel and then serve with the pasta mixture.

Garnish with fresh oregano and cheese.

Slow-Cooked Chicken Stew with Gnocchi

Prep: 15 minutes
Cook: 6 to 8 hours 2 minutes (low) / 4 to 5 hours (high)

Ingredients:
5 oz fresh baby spinach
2 to 3 cloves garlic
6 slices bacon
2 1lb mini potato gnocchi
2 12 oz cans evaporated milk
2 Tbsp cornstarch dissolved in 2 Tbsp water
4 cups chicken broth
1 tsp salt
1 tsp poultry seasoning
1 to 2 tsp Italian seasoning
1 to 2 tsp dried basil
2 cups mixed carrots, celery, and onions
1 lb skinless, boneless, chicken breasts

Instructions:
In a slow cooker, add the chicken, 2 cups mixed carrots, celery, and onions, seasonings, broth, and salt. Slow-cook accordingly (refer to times stated above).

Add evaporated milk, cornstarch mixture, and gnocchi. Stir and bring the cover back.

Fry bacon until crispy and sauté with garlic for at least a minute. Add to the slow cooker and stir to combine.

Add more liquid, if desired.

Season with salt and pepper, to taste.

Slow-Cooked Chocolate Cherry Lava Cake

Prep: 15 minutes
Cook: 3 hours

Ingredients:
2 cups semi-sweet chocolate chips
1 cup instant chocolate pudding mix
2 cups cold 2% milk
1/3 cup canola oil
3 large eggs
1 2/3 cup water
1 pack devil's food cake mix (regular size)

Instructions:
Combine cake mix, eggs, water, and oil in a bowl and then beat on low for at least 30 seconds.

Continue beating cake mix in medium for at least 2 minutes and then transfer into 4 quart slow-cooker.

Whisk pudding mix and milk in a bowl for 2 minutes and let stand until soft-set. Spoon over cake batter and add chocolate chips on top and cook for 3 to 4 hour hours, or until moist.

Serve warm and enjoy!

Pulled Pork and Butternut Squash Tacos

Prep: 15 minutes
Cook: 7 hours, 40 minutes

Ingredients:
2 Tbsp Jalapeno Red Wine Vinegar
½ cup orange juice
2 tsp minced garlic
1 onion, chopped coarsely
 2 Tbsp adobo sauce
2/3 canned chipotle in adobo sauce
1 Tbsp olive oil
1 tsp ground cinnamon
1 tsp ground cumin
1 tsp black pepper
2 tsp kosher salt, divided
2 lbs boneless pork loin roast
3 lbs butternut squash, cut into bite-size chunks
Corn tortillas, feta cheese, lime wedges (for serving)

Instructions:
Place the squash in the bottom of the slow-cooker and add some salt.

Season pork with pepper and remaining salt and then add cinnamon, cumin, adobo sauce, chipotle chilis, and olive oil and make sure to rub these all over the meat. Place garlic and onion on top and then add red wine vinegar and orange.

Cover and cook for around 6 to 8 hours or until meat is cooked thoroughly and tender. Shred the pork and place in a large bowl before removing onions and squash. Toss with pork to combine.

Microwave the tortillas and place what you have made inside.

Serve and enjoy!

Slow-Cooked Special Poached Salmon

Prep: 10 minutes
Cook: 1 to 1 ½ hour

Ingredients:
Kosher salt and freshly ground black pepper
2 lbs salmon fillets, skin-on
1 tsp kosher salt
1 tsp black peppercorns
5 to 6 sprigs of fresh herbs of your choice
1 bay leaf
1 shallot, sliced thinly
1 lemon, sliced thinly
1 cup dry white wine
2 cups water

Instructions:
Combine shallots, water, lemon, wine, peppercorns, herbs, bay leaf and salt together in the slow-cooker and cook for at least 30 minutes on high.
Use salt and pepper to season salmon with before placing skin-side down on the slow-cooker. Cover until salmon is opaque and flaky and cook for 45 minutes to 1 hour.
Serve drizzled with olive oil and fresh lemon juice.
Serve and enjoy!

Chapter 2: Transforming Leftovers

Next, it's time to learn how to make something good out of leftovers! Say you have leftover turkey, or ham, or anything from certain celebrations. It wouldn't be right to just throw them away, would it? So, of course, what you can do is make sure that you turn them into delicious recipes—and you'll learn about that in this chapter.

Slow-Cooked Turkey Tetrazinni

Prep: 15 minutes
Cook: 4 hours, 15 minutes

Ingredients:
2 cups cooked turkey breast, diced
½ cup heavy cream
1 cup chicken or vegetable broth
1 can cream of mushroom or chicken soup
A pinch of nutmeg
½ tsp pepper
½ tsp salt
¼ tsp paprika
1 tsp dried parsley
1 jar sliced mushrooms, drained
2 Tbsp pimientos, chopped
¼ cup white onions, chopped
1 cup parmesan cheese, shredded
1 cup frozen peas
2 cups spaghetti noodles, broken and uncooked
¼ cup dry white wine

Instructions:
Spray some cooking spray on the bottom of a slow-cooker.

Stir soup, cream, whine, and broth in a large bowl.

Then, add noodles, turkey, peas, nutmeg, salt, pepper, paprika, parsley, mushrooms, pimientos, onion, and cheese. Stir until well-combined.

Pour into a slow-cooker and top with Parmesan cheese.

Cover and then cook as needed.

Serve topped with salt and parsley, and more cheese, if you want.

Slow-Cooked Breakfast Casserole

Prep: 10 minutes
Cook: 10 to 12 hours (overnight)

Ingredients:
1 tsp black pepper
1 tsp salt
1 cup skim milk
12 eggs
1 ½ cup shredded cheese
1 green bell pepper, diced
1 onion, diced
1 lb lean cooked ham, diced
32 oz hash browns

Instructions:
Spray cooking oil on the slow-cooker.

Add cheese, vegetables, ham, and potatoes. Try to make several layers out of them in the crockpot. You can do this by starting with the hash browns. Then, add the ham, followed by onions, peppers, and finally, some cheese. Repeat until you have made several layers.

Beat milk, eggs, salt, and pepper in the slow cooker and cook on low.

Serve for breakfast and enjoy!

Slow-Cooked Leftover Pork Roast Ragu

Prep: 15 minutes
Cook: 6 to 8 hours

Ingredients:
leftover roasted pork (can use chicken or turkey)
Pasta (your choice)
2 small cans of tomato paste (depending on consistency desired)
2 smoked bacon strips
½ red pepper, deseeded and diced finely
1 onion, diced finely
1 carrot, peeled and diced finely
1 celery stick, chopped finely

Instructions:
Add vegetables in the basin of the slow-cooker.

Add bacon and meat.

Then, add the pasta and the herbs.

Put the lid on and cook until tender—or for 6 to 8 hours, or just until tender.

Serve with Parmesan cheese, your choice of pasta, or rice, if desired.

Enjoy!

Slow-Cooked Turkey, Lemon, and Couscous Soup

Prep: 15 minutes
Cook: 8 ½ hours

Ingredients:
1 ½ cups cooked turkey meat, dark and light
2 cooked turkey wings, skin and bones intact
1 stalk celery, chopped finely
1 large carrot, peeled and chopped finely
1 Tbsp olive oil
¼ cup flat-leaf parsley
¼ cup Israeli couscous
Kosher salt and ground black pepper
1 cup dry white wine
6 cups low-sodium turkey or chicken stock
1 Tbsp Worcestershire sauce
½ lemon
¼ tsp poultry seasoning
3 sprigs fresh thyme
2 bay leaves
2 cloves garlic, minced
1 medium onion, chopped finely
1 large carrot, chopped finely

Instructions:
Put turkey meat and wings in the bottom of the slow-cooker.

Then, heat some oil in a medium or Dutch oven. Add vegetables and cook until they start to soften. Stir in onion, celery, and carrot. Add garlic and stir some more or for at least a minute.

Add vegetables and bay leaves to the slow-cooker. Add thyme, lemon, and poultry seasoning, together with wine, stock, and Worcestershire sauce. Season with salt and pepper to taste, and cook as needed.

Take the turkey off the slow-cooker and take the meat away from the bones. Discard bones and skin and bring the meat back to the slow-cooker. Add couscous and cook for another hour and a half longer.

Discard the bay leaves, and then add half of the lemon together with thyme sprigs.

Add seasonings, to taste.

Serve in bowls and enjoy!

Slow-Cooked Ham and White Bean Soup

Prep: 15 minutes
Cook: 8 hours

Ingredients:
2 Tbsp parsley leaves, chopped
Kosher salt and freshly ground black pepper, to taste
2 bay leaves
¼ tsp dried rosemary
½ tsp dried oregano
2 cans white beans, drained and rinsed
2 celery stalks, diced
3 carrots, peeled and diced
1 onion, diced
2 cloves garlic, minced
2 cups leftover ham, diced
1 leftover hambone (may substitute any other meat)

Instructions:
Put the meat, garlic, ham, bay leaves, rosemary, oregano, white beans, celery, carrots, and onions into the slow cooker. Add 6 cups of water, salt, and pepper, and stir until well combined.

Cover and cook on high for at least 7 to 8 hours.

Serve immediately and top with parsley or cheese.

Enjoy!

Chapter 3: Recipes for 3 to 3 ½ quart Slow Cookers

Then, there are also recipes that are meant for 3 to 3 ½ quart slow cookers—which, as you may have noticed, are smaller than standard-sized ones. For that, here are the recipes you could make.

Slow-Cooked Spaghetti and Meatballs

Prep: 5 minutes
Cook: 5 to 7 hours

Ingredients:
8 frozen turkey meatballs
1 cup spaghetti sauce
4 oz uncooked thin spaghetti
1 cup water

Instructions:
Spray some cooking oil inside the slow-cooker.

Combine water and sauce in the slow-cooker before adding the meatballs and then cook on low for 5 to 7 hours.

Serve with garlic bread on the side and enjoy!

Slow-Cooked Apple Cinnamon Oatmeal

Prep: 10 minutes
Cook: 8 to 9 hours (overnight)

Ingredients:
A dash of salt
2 cups water
1 cup old-fashioned rolled oats
2 Tbsp plus 2 tsp brown sugar
½ tsp cinnamon
1 apple, peeled and sliced

Instructions:
First, make sure to slice the apples before placing them in the bottom of the slow-cooker.

Add cinnamon and brown sugar, and stir until well-combined. Add oats and water, and mix.

Cook overnight or for at least 8 to 9 hours.

Stir well, and serve.

Slow-Cooked Salsa Cheesy Chicken Soup

Prep: 5 minutes
Cook: 6 to 8 hours

Ingredients:
¼ cup light sour cream
1 ½ tsp taco seasoning
½ can cheddar cheese soup
½ cup salsa
2 skinless and boneless chicken breast halves

Instructions:
Put chicken in the bottom of the slow-cooker and then add seasoning over the chicken. Add cheese and salsa in a bowl and pour this mixture over the chicken, and cook as needed (see above).

Use potholders to remove the stoneware from the slow-cooker before adding sour cream.

Serve as enchilada filling, or with rice, if desired.

Slow-Cooked Beef Stroganoff

Prep: 10 minutes
Cook: 8 hours, 10 minutes

Ingredients:
1 ½ cups cooked rice or noodles
½ cup sour cream
1/8 tsp pepper
1 jar mushrooms, drained
1 can condensed mushroom soup
¼ cup onion, chopped
½ lb beef stew meat

Instructions:
Add beef, soup, pepper, and mushrooms in the bottom of the slow-cooker.

Cover and cook until beef is tender, or for around 6 to 8 hours.

Add sour cream and stir shortly before serving.

Serve and enjoy!

Slow-Cooked Chickpea and Vegetable Curry

Prep: 5 minutes
Cook: 5 to 6 hours

Ingredients:
Cooked brown rice
¼ cup fresh basil leaves, shredded
1 14 oz can light coconut milk
2 to 3 tsp curry powder
1 14 oz can vegetable broth
½ cup chopped onion
1 cup sliced carrots
1 cup loose-pack frozen green cut beans
1 15 oz can chickpeas, drained and rinsed
3 cups cauliflower florets

Instructions:
Combine cauliflower florets, green beans, onion, carrots, and chickpeas in the bottom of the slow-cooker before adding curry powder and broth.

Cook for at least 5 to 6 hours before adding shredded basil leaves and coconut milk.

Spoon rice on top and serve.

Enjoy!

Chapter 4: Gluten, Vegan, Soy, and Nut-Free Options

Of course, if you're going to cook healthy, you have to think about gluten, nut, or soy-free dishes, as well as vegan recipes that you can serve, especially if you have guests in the said categories. For these, you can try the following recipes:

Gluten-Free Caramel Flan

Prep: 15 minutes
Cook: 2 hours, 15 minutes

Ingredients:
14 oz can condensed milk, sweetened
14 oz 2% milk
Whipped cream
5 Tbsp caramel sauce
3 eggs

Instructions:
Mix regular milk, condensed milk, and eggs in a medium bowl and whisk until milk is no longer heavy—or until it settles in the bottom of the bowl.

Arrange some ramekins and add caramel sauce into each of them. Add milk up to the inner lip and stack up to 5 ramekins in the slow-cooker.

Cover and cook for at least 2 hours or until flan has puffed.

Remove the flans from the cooker and serve with some whipped cream.

Enjoy!

Gluten-Free Coconut Granola Bars

Prep: 10 minutes
Cook: 2 ½ hours

Ingredients:

2 flax eggs
4 to 5 medjool dates, chopped
½ tsp sea salt
½ tsp baking powder
2 Tbsp chia seeds
2 tsp ground vanilla beans
¼ cup sweetened coconut, shredded
¼ cup flax meal
½ cup coconut butter
½ cup maple syrup
½ cup gluten-free rolled oats

Instructions:

Combine all of the ingredients in a bowl, and then combine the wet ingredients in another bowl.

Fold the chopped dates in before greasing the slow-cooker and make sure to put parchment paper in the bottom of the slow cooker.

Add batter into the slow cooker and pat until well-distributed and then cook on low for at least 2 ½ hours.

Pull out the bars once they're done and let cool for at least 40 minutes before serving.

Enjoy!

Chicken Chili Verde

Prep: 10 minutes
Cook: 6 to 8 hours

Ingredients:
Salt and pepper, to taste
½ cup fresh cilantro
1 tsp ground coriander
1 dried bay leaf
1 red bell pepper, diced
½ large onion, diced
4 to 5 lb organic pasture raised whole chicken
2 cups water
3 cups salsa verde

Instructions:
Pat the chicken dry on paper towels or on a clean work surface. Cut excess skin and fat.

Add two cups of liquid and salsa verde to the slow cooker before adding bell pepper, onion, bay leaf, fresh cilantro, and ground coriander. Stir and cook for 6 to 8 hours.

After cooking, take the chicken away from the slow-cooker and take off the meat from the bones. Use two forks to shred it and serve after ladling it into bowls.

Gluten-Free Mandarin Chicken Thighs

Prep: 10 minutes
Cook: 6 hours

Ingredients:
2 Tbsp fish sauce
1 tsp sesame oil
1 Tbsp granulated sugar substitute
1 Tbsp lime juice
½ tsp red chili, sliced
1 Tbsp minced ginger
1 tsp minced garlic
1 cup no sugar added Mandarin Orange Slices
½ tsp kosher salt
1 Tbsp Chinese Five Spice Powder
6 chicken thighs

Instructions:
Use five spice powder and salt to rub chicken thighs with. Sear the chicken skin-side down for around 3 minutes over high heat and then add all of the ingredients for the sauce.

Cook for around 6 hours on high—or 4 on low, and then transfer the chicken to a shallow dish. Pour remaining sauce into blender with the xanthan gum and blend for at least 20 seconds and then pour on the chicken platter.

Serve topped with cilantro and enjoy!

Vegan Puttanesca Pasta

Prep: 15 minutes
Cook: 1 hour 45 minutes

Ingredients:
½ cup vegan mozzarella cheese, shredded
Salt and freshly ground black pepper, to taste
¼ tsp red hot pepper flakes
¼ tsp sugar
¼ tsp garlic powder
¼ tsp dried oregano
¼ tsp dried basil
1 Tbsp fresh flat-leaf parsley, chopped
1 Tbsp capers, drained and rinsed
¼ cup pitted green olives, sliced
¼ cup pitted kalamata olives, sliced
½ cup crushed tomatoes
½ cup warm water
1 Tbsp olive oil
½ tsp Italian Seasoning
½ tsp salt
1 ½ tsp instant yeast
1 ½ cups unbleached all-purpose flour

Instructions:

Oil a bowl while pulsing flour, Italian Seasoning, yeast, and salt in the food processor. Add some more oil to the feed tube and pulse again.

Transfer the dough to a floured surface and knead for at least a minute or two before shaping it into a ball—like you would a regular pizza. Cover with plastic wrap and set aside.

Make the sauce by mixing the wet ingredients together and season with salt and pepper, to taste.

Punch the dough down and add vegan mozzarella.

Cook for 1 hour and 30 minutes and serve immediately.

Italian Eggplant Casserole with Tofu-Cashew Ricotta

Prep: 20 minutes
Cook: 8 hours

Ingredients:
For the biscuits:
1 ½ cup plain, unsweetened non-dairy milk
3 Tbsp olive oil
1 ½ tsp baking powder
½ tsp dried thyme
½ tsp salt
1 cup white gluten-free flour
For the stew:
2 Tbsp coconut flour
Salt and pepper, to taste
1 tsp dried thyme
2 Tbsp vegan bouillon
1 cup water (or as needed)
10 oz sliced mushrooms
1 lb frozen mixed vegetables
1 ½ cups cubed chicken-flavored vegan sausage
1 large stalk celery, minced
1 small onion, minced

Instructions:

Put some oil on the slow cooker and add all of the stew ingredients in, with the exception of the flour. Add more water, if needed, and cook for 8 hours.

Make the biscuits by means of combining all of the ingredients in a bowl until you form a dough and cut using rim of a glass.

Bake the tofu in a preheated oven (475 F), and then drain before cutting into cubes. Bake for 25 to 30 minutes until crisp and browned.

Serve and enjoy!

Indian Spiced Lentils

Prep: 15 minutes
Cook: 3 ½ hours

Ingredients:
Salt and pepper, to taste
Juice of 1 lemon
2/3 cup vegetable broth
1 tsp garam masala
1 Tbsp ground coriander
2 tsp paprika
¼ tsp cayenne
2 tsp ground cumin
½ tsp ground ginger
1 15 oz can tomato sauce
3 to 4 cloves garlic, diced finely
1 yellow bell pepper, diced finely
1 sweet potato, peeled and diced finely
2 ½ cups lentils, cooked

Instructions:
Place all of the ingredients in the crock pot and then cook on high for 3 hours. Add more potatoes, if desired, and cook for 30 minutes more.

Serve with Naan bread or brown rice, if desired.

Enjoy!

Tofu Teriyaki with Rice and Kale

Prep: 15 minutes
Cook: 2 to 3 hours

Ingredients:
Fresh, shredded kale
Rice
6 fresh or canned pineapple rings
3 to 4 cloves of garlic, minced finely or grated
1 Tbsp grated ginger
1 Tbsp sesame oil
2 Tbsp brown sugar
¼ cup unsweetened rice vinegar
¼ cup mirin
½ cup tamari sauce
½ cup vegetable broth
1 cup pineapple juice
2 1lb packs extra firm tofu

Instructions:
First, drain the tofu and cut into rectangular slices. Press to remove excess water and then set aside.

Whisk tamari, juice, vinegar, sugar, oil, garlic, and ginger in a bowl and then put pineapple juice in the casserole dish. Top with tofu triangles and bake at 325 degrees for 2 to 3 hours.

Serve over a bed of rice and kale and enjoy!

Chapter 5: Cooking for Couples in the Kitchen

Finally, here are the best dishes you can make for couples! These are perfect for dinner dates, or just spending time with a loved one!

Slow Cooked White Turkey Chili

Prep: 10 minutes
Cook: 4 hours

Ingredients:
2 avocados, pitted and cut into ½ inch pieces
1 tsp pepper
1 tsp salt
2 lbs leftover turkey meat, shredded
3 cans cannellini beans, drained and rinsed
2 tsp ground coriander
4 tsp ground cumin
6 garlic cloves, minced
4 jalapenos, stemmed, seeded, and minced
1 cup onions, chopped
2 Tbsp vegetable oil
1 can white or yellow hominy, drained and rinsed
3 cups low sodium turkey stock

Instructions:
Puree 2 cups of turkey stock in a blender together with the hominy, and then pour contents into the bottom of a slow-cooker.

Set the heat to medium-high and then add oil, jalapenos, and onions. Add coriander, cumin, and garlic, and stir until tender. Add the remaining turkey stock that you have with you, and then pour contents into the slow-cooker again.

Add turkey meat, beans, pepper, and salt and stir everything together.

Cover the slow-cooker and cook for 4 hours, on low.

Serve topped with cilantro and avocado.

Slow-Cooked Chicken Fajitas

Prep: 5 minutes
Cook: 6 hours

Ingredients:
½ tsp ground black pepper
½ tsp kosher salt
1 tsp ground cumin
1 ½ tsp chili powder
2 large chicken breasts
1 cup salsa
Juice of 1 lime
3 garlic cloves, minced
1 large onion, sliced into half-moons
5 bell peppers, sliced
½ cup chicken stock

Instructions:
Place the chicken inside the slow-cooker.

Add the remaining ingredients and then place chicken breasts on top.

Add salt, cumin, chili powder, pepper, and salt, and then cook until chicken shreds, or for at least 5 to 6 hours.

Take the chicken off the cooker after the given time.

Shred the chicken and together with the remaining ingredients, put it back in the cooker.

Serve and enjoy!

Slow-Cooked Korean Tacos

Prep: 10 minutes
Cook: 9 hours

Ingredients:
Brown rice or small tortillas (for serving)
2 Tbsp brown sugar
3 Tbsp rice wine vinegar
1 16-oz pack of broccoli or coleslaw mix
3 tsp ground ginger
3 green onions (more for garnish)
3 garlic cloves, minced
1 cup hoisin sauce
2 lbs boneless pork loin, cut into 4 pieces

Instructions:
Add pork into the slow-cooker and add green onions, hoisin sauce, ground ginger, and garlic. Add pork to the spices and sauce and toss until pork is fully-coated.

Cover and cook on low for at least 8 to 9 hours.

Toss some coleslaw with brown sugar and wine vinegar.

Shred pork after removing from slow-cooker and then bring it back into the sauce. Toss to coat.

Serve on a bed of rice, or with tortillas. Garnish with sliced onions, as well.

Slow-Cooked Mississippi Roast

Prep: 5 minutes
Cook: 8 hours

Ingredients:
5-6 pepperoncini
¼ cup water
6 Tbsp unsalted water
1 1 oz pack of dry au jus gravy mix
1 1 oz pack of dry ranch seasoning mix
1 3 lb chuck roast

Instructions:
Put the chuck roast in the bottom of the slow-cooker after adding ¼ cup of water.

Add dry ranch seasoning on the chuck roast together with dry au jus gravy mix, butter, and pepperoncini.

Cook for around 8 hours and then serve with gravy.

Serve and enjoy!

Slow-Cooked Corn Chowder

Prep: 5 minutes
Cook: 8 hours

Ingredients:
2 cups half and half
¼ cup unsalted butter
2 tsp black pepper
2 tsp salt
1 large onion, diced
8 oz diced pancetta
2 cups low sodium chicken broth
1 can whole kernel corn
1 can cream of corn
6 potatoes, peeled and diced

Instructions:
Put potatoes in the bottom of the slow-cooker, together with onion, pancetta, chicken broth, corn kernels, and cream of corn.

Cook until potatoes are fork-tender, or for at least 7 hours.

Add butter and half and half before cooking for another 30 minutes.

Serve and enjoy!

Slow-Cooked Chicken Tikka Masala

Prep: 15 minutes
Cook: 8 hours

Ingredients:
Chopped cilantro or parsley
Lemon juice
Half of 1 lemon
3 Tbsp cornstarch
1 cup heavy cream
2 bay leaves
1 to 3 tsp cayenne pepper
¾ tsp ground black pepper
¾ tsp cinnamon
2 tsp salt (or to taste)
½ Tbsp paprika
1 Tbsp cumin
1 tsp turmeric powder
2 Tbsp masala
2 Tbsp olive oil
1 ½ cups plain yogurt
1 can tomato puree
2 Tbsp fresh ginger, minced
4 cloves garlic, minced
1 large onion, diced

Instructions:

Place chicken in the bottom of the slow-cooker, together with cayenne pepper, black pepper, cinnamon, salt, paprika, cumin, turmeric powder, garam masala, olive oil, yogurt, tomato puree, ginger, and garlic. Add two bay leaves.

Cover and cook for 4 hours on low, and 8 hours on high.

Whisk corn starch and heavy cream in a bowl and then pour the mixture into the slow-cooker. Cook for at least 20 minutes more to let it thicken and then squeeze half a lemon into it.

Serve on a bed of brown rice while it's hot, and enjoy!

Slow-Cooked Mini Pork Sliders

Prep: 5 minutes
Cook: 6 hours

Ingredients:
1 cup BBQ sauce
1 12 oz can of soda
2 lbs pork shoulder, tenderloin, or butt

Instructions:
Place pork inside the slow-cooker and pour some soda on top of the fork.

Cook on low for around 6 hours.

Put pork on cutting board after cooking and cool for 5 minutes. Discard liquid from slow-cooker.

Shred pork and put it back in the slow-cooker before coating with barbecue sauce.

Serve on toasted buns and enjoy!

Slow-Cooked Chorizo, Two Bean Chili, and Potatoes

Prep: 10 minutes
Cook: 6 hours

Ingredients:
2 ¾ cups chicken stock
1 tsp kosher salt, more to taste
1 tsp tomato paste
1 tsp ground cumin
1 tsp chili powder
2 garlic cloves, minced
1 medium onion, diced
4 oz can sliced jalapenos
2 14.5 oz cans fire roasted tomatoes, undrained
1 can pinto beans, drained and rinsed
1 can black beans, drained and rinsed
3 cups diced potatoes
½ lb chorizo sausage, casings removed

Instructions:
Break and brown the chorizo in a skillet and then place it in the slow-cooker.

Add more of the ingredients into the slow-cooker. Cook for at least four to six hours on low.

Add more chili and chicken stock.

Serve topped with grated cheddar cheese and enjoy!

Slow-Cooked Chicken Adobo

Prep: 10 minutes
Cook: 6 hours, 30 minutes

Ingredients:
2 lbs chicken thighs, excess fat removed
¼ cup apple cider vinegar
½ cup low-sodium soy sauce
½ cup chicken stock
2 bay leaves
¼ tsp cayenne powder
½ tsp ground black pepper
3 Tbsp dark brown sugar
6 cloves of garlic, minced
2 shallots, minced
1 tsp olive oil

Instructions:
Rub some oil inside the slow-cooker before adding black pepper, bay leaves, cayenne pepper, brown sugar, garlic, and shallots.

Add chicken stock, apple cider vinegar, and soy sauce and then use spoon to stir everything together. Make sure everything's been distributed equally.

Add chicken thighs and spoon some sauce on top and then cook on low for at least 6 hours.

Prepare a baking sheet with aluminum foil and place chicken inside the slow-cooker. Strain the sauce into pot and cook for at least 20 to 30 minutes more. Add more cornstarch if you feel like the sauce has not thickened properly.

Brush sauce over the chicken and make sure it's well-coated.

Serve and enjoy!

Conclusion

Thank you for reading this book!

Hopefully, this book has inspired you to make slow-cooked dishes that you can serve to your loved one, and even know healthier substitutes that you can use for the dishes you'll be making!

Make sure that you try the recipes given here to see which suit your taste the best. After all, practice makes perfect. Cook some now, and for sure, you'll be cooking even better in time.

Finally, if you enjoyed this book, please take time to post a review on Amazon. It will be greatly appreciated.

Thank you, and good luck!

Thank you again for downloading this book!

I hope this book was able to help you to successfully complete the Daniel Fast!

The next step is to check out my other book: *Slow Cooker Recipes: Best Simple and Deliciously Healthy Recipes for 2016*", I'm sure it will help you to cook healthy and make great meals on the go!

Finally, if you enjoyed this book, then I'd like to ask you for a favor, would you be kind enough to leave a review for this book on Amazon? It'd be greatly appreciated!

Click here to leave a review for this book on Amazon!

Thank you and good luck!

Preview Of 'Slow Cooker Recipes: New for 2016'

Chapter 1. Daniel Fast Shopping List

You must always remember that the line between allowed and forbidden is quite thin for the Daniel Fast diet. Just take salt as an example. Iodized, rock or other salty additives to food are banned in this diet. However, you may use the Himalayan salt during the Daniel Fast. This kind of salt has natural elements that are known to regulate water in the body. It also promotes the pH level of the cells among other things.

In the Old Testament, Adam and Eve were advised not to eat the forbidden fruit. The Daniel Fast allows this fruit but it does not agree with the consumption of dairy, sugar, meat, bread, oil, alcohol and coffee. Eggs and yeast are also included in the foods to avoid.

Patience and determination is needed to succeed in a Daniel Fast diet. It is now time to say goodbye to the sinful foods that you have grown up with. For a stronger and healthier you, here is your guide to bring with when you go to the grocery store to buy the ingredients for your 21 day menu. Keep in mind that you are not to buy everything right away since it is your option to choose the right kind of meals within the Daniel Fast that you will prepare for a certain day.

Vegetables (all kinds in frozen, cooked or raw form)
Fruits (all kinds in cooked, fresh, dried or frozen form)
Drinks
> Water
> Coconut water
> Almond milk
> Vegetable juice
> Coconut kefir

Legumes and Beans (all kinds that are cooked and dried)
Seeds and Nuts (all kinds that are dry roasted, raw or sprouted) *unsalted
Whole grain (flour, bread or wheat is not permitted)
> Millet
> Buckwheat
> Quinoa
> Barley
> Brown rice
> Sourdough (this is the only bread allowed)
> Whole grain pasta (allowed but not liberally consumed)

Chapter 2. Daniel Fast Benefits and Frequently Asked Questions

It is clear that there are several benefits you can receive from the Daniel Fast but at the end of the day, you need to know that it should begin with being motivated spiritually. It is chronicled in the Bible, in Isaiah 58:6, that when you "loose the bonds of wickedness" your soul shall be set free. That is why this diet will provide your body with the following:

- Addiction to meat, dairy and sugar is lessened
- Anxiety is lessened
- Brain fog is decreased
- High cholesterol levels are decreased
- Depression and lethargy is lessened
- Gradual weight loss is promoted
- Energy levels are increased
- Toxins in the body are eliminated
- Hormonal levels are normalized
- Skin conditions are normalized

In starting the Daniel Fast, it is always advised by physicians to get tested for ailments that may interfere should it interact with certain medications. If you are a woman, it is necessary to check if you are pregnant or nursing. If you are on a special diet that requires you to consume food that is high in protein and carbohydrates, then the Daniel Fast is not for you.

In the event you are not in the red flag category as stated above, then congratulations! The Daniel Fast is the perfect diet for you to consider. By now, you have a lot of questions running through your mind. Majority of the dieters who would want to try the Daniel Fast have asked similar questions like you do right now.

For your reference, here are the most frequently asked questions.

FAQ #1: Meat is not allowed in this diet so where can I source my protein requirements?

Worry not that the Daniel Fast prohibits the consumption of meat in your diet. There are other sources of food that have the same or even higher levels of protein! Do eat lentils, brown rice, quinoa and almonds. You can still receive your dose of protein from these food items.

FAQ #2: During my fasting, am I stuck with eating the food I prepare at home? Does it mean I cannot dine in restaurants anymore?

Try not to associate fasting as if it were the end of the world. With the Daniel Fast, you may eat at your favorite restaurants for as long as you specifically order plain baked potatoes. When it comes to salad, go ahead and indulge; you are allowed to eat them for as long as they are dressed in olive oil.

FAQ #3: I cannot live without bread! You mean to say this fasting is made up of just fruits and plants?

You need to understand that the Daniel Fast started more than 2,000 years ago. This means that grains were only limited to a handful species. Right now, you may consider the sourdough bread.

FAQ #4: What are the Daniel Fast guidelines I have to follow? Are they super strict that I faint with thirst and hunger?

The Daniel Fast is not at all depriving you from living, so do not get so paranoid. This way of fasting is all about denying yourself of the food you have immensely consumed in the past. When you feel hungry, stop for a while and put yourself in the presence of the Lord. Praying and focusing on the word of God will give you enlightenment on the right things to do in life. The Do's and Don'ts of eating are guides for you to follow in order to achieve the results you are aiming for.

FAQ #5: Can I eat seafood while on the Daniel Fast?

No. Mussels from shells, shrimps and fish are considered as meat. The Daniel Fast is this generation's contribution to the Christian faith that complies with the morals of vegetarianism in order to strengthen one's mind and body.

Looking back, the same morals were prominent in abstaining from eating meat as stated in Daniel 10:1-2 *"In those days I, Daniel, was mourning three full weeks. [I ate] No pleasant food, no meat or wine came into my mouth; nor did I anoint myself at all, until three whole weeks were fulfilled."*

You can still feel stronger and full when you eat soy-based food. They are allowed in the Daniel Fast. If at first you fail, just keep praying for strength and in a couple of days, you shall prevail.

Don't forget to like Slow Cooker Meals For Two on Facebook!

https://www.facebook.com/Slowcookingfortwo/

To purchase the next book in this series:
"Daniel Fast: The Ultimate Guide to Slow Cooker Meals for Breakfast, Lunch, and Dinner for 2016 - Dairy Free & Vegan", **click <u>HERE</u>**

www.ingramcontent.com/pod-product-compliance
Lightning Source LLC
Chambersburg PA
CBHW061159040426
42445CB00013B/1729